the ART of Making Things Happen in Your Life

the ART *of* Making Things Happen in Your Life

Dean Drawbaugh

DESTINY IMAGE® PUBLISHERS, INC.
PO Box 310, Shippensburg, PA 17257-0310

"Speaking to the Purposes of God for This Generation and for the Generations to Come."

This book and all other Destiny Image, Revival Press, Mercy Place, Fresh Bread, Destiny Image Fiction, and Treasure House books are available at Christian bookstores and distributors worldwide.

For a U.S. bookstore nearest you, call 1-800-722-6774.
For more information on foreign distributors, call 717-532-3040.
Or reach us on the Internet: www.destinyimage.com

ISBN 10: 0-7684-3864-0
ISBN 13: 978-0-7684-3864-2

For Worldwide Distribution, Printed in the U.S.A.
1 2 3 4 5 6 / 14 13 12 11

Acknowledgments

I would like to thank all the people who send me wonderful e-mail stories. A good illustration makes a lesson easier to learn.

To all dedicated people who mentored me through life's lessons. Thank you for your precious time and wise counsel.

I thank my parents for instilling in me the habits that have made me successful. You see, I was listening!

I especially thank my darling wife, Phyllis, who loves me for who I am and makes life worth living.

Humor helps us think outside the box.

It's been said that the average child laughs about 400 times per day, while the average adult laughs only 25 times per day.

What happens to the other 375 laughs?

I guess that's why most of us are still in the box!

Contents

Section III
Organize for Opportunity

Section IV
Prepare Your Team for Opportunity

Preface

Chart Your Course

The following is the transcript of an actual radio conversation of a U.S. naval ship with Canadian authorities off the coast of Newfoundland in October 1995 that was released by the Chief of Naval Operations on November 10, 1995.

Americans: Please divert your course 15 degrees to the North to avoid a collision.

Canadians: Recommend you divert YOUR course 15 degrees to the South to avoid a collision.

Americans: This is the Captain of a US Navy ship. I say again, divert YOUR course.

Canadians: No. I say again, you divert YOUR course.

Americans: THIS IS THE AIRCRAFT CARRIER USS LINCOLN, THE SECOND LARGEST SHIP IN THE UNITED STATES' ATLANTIC FLEET. WE ARE ACCOMPANIED BY THREE DESTROYERS, THREE CRUISERS, AND NUMEROUS SUPPORT VESSELS. I DEMAND THAT YOU CHANGE YOUR COURSE 15 DEGREES NORTH, THAT'S ONE FIVE DEGREES NORTH, OR COUNTER-MEASURES WILL BE UNDERTAKEN TO ENSURE THE SAFETY OF THIS SHIP.

Canadians: This is a lighthouse. Your call!

ON COURSE

Are you on course toward your destiny? Or are you heading toward the rocky shoreline of a lighthouse? This book provides four distinct tools to chart your course toward making good things happen in your life.

First, each of the twelve chapters focuses on specific characteristics, actions, or traits that will help propel you toward achieving your goals in your family, career, relationships, business, ministry, and all aspects of your life. These concepts help you focus on the person you would like to become—an optimistic, successful person ready to take advantage of the next exciting opportunity that life presents to you. This is your planned destination.

Second, each chapter includes four Self Assessment Questions. Being honest with yourself while answering these questions helps you determine what you were doing right and what you need to improve. If you seriously complete all 52 questions, you will have a good idea of what your journey will look like—and that you will achieve your dreams, aspirations, and destiny.

Third, at the end of each chapter you are asked to provide a self-evaluation pinpointing where you feel you are now. Always remember that it doesn't matter if you are a one or a ten—what matters is that you recognize where you are right now. Identifying where you are and determining where you want to go from here allows you to plan your journey, rather than having no control and just moving along with the current.

Finally, and most important, a call to action—or things to do list—to plan your next step and get you moving. Nothing will happen in your life until you do something.

Introduction

Rethinking Your Life Strategy

Everyone remembers the story of the tortoise and the hare—the rabbit gets a fast start and builds a big lead, but loses interest quickly. The turtle, on the other hand, plods along slow but steady and eventually overtakes the resting rabbit to win the race.

At the beginning of the story we tend to identify with the rabbit. Most people envision themselves as the fastest, strongest, and most attractive. There is no doubt that you know people like the rabbit who have a seemingly endless supply of great ideas, but none ever get thought through to completion.

At the end of the tortoise and hare story, most people tend to identify with the turtle. After all, being industrious and winning is better than being lazy and losing. There is no doubt that you know people who, like the turtle, plod along day to day, steady as a rock, finishing the race whatever the cost. These are the people who show up every day, work hard, and grind out a living.

Stress is the difference between where you are and where you think you should be.

The story of the tortoise and the hare paints a black and white picture to illustrate a point. However in real life, both the turtle and the rabbit would experience stress as they fail to reach their potential.

The turtle would experience stress because he is not achieving most of his goals—his vision is too narrow. The rabbit would experience stress because his plans are bigger than his current resources will allow, so he is destined to fail—unless his competition also lays down to rest on the way to the finish line.

Capitalize on your strengths, minimize your weaknesses.

What if the turtle would rethink his strategy—for instance, most turtles are faster than rabbits are in water. If the turtle could schedule the race to be in the water, it would give him an advantage right from the beginning of the race. Capitalizing on this strength allows the turtle to get ahead and finish ahead. This new strategy is equivalent to a person rethinking how working hard at the wrong tasks doesn't give enough traction, needed to get ahead. Taking inventory of the person's strengths and using them to his or her advantage advances the person toward the goal.

The rabbit had the advantage of speed at the beginning of the race, but he didn't pace himself for the entire distance. If the rabbit would rethink his strategy, he would shorten the course. Planning for his attention span weakness would allow him to get ahead and finish ahead. This is equivalent to the person who continually takes on more work than is possible to complete on deadline. Consequently, the many opportunities presented to the person end up being judged on the incomplete projects rather than what is completed correctly and on time.

As different as the tortoise and the hare are in their strengths and weaknesses, there is a strategy that would have allowed each of them to excel. The same is true for you. You can be successful today with the right approach.

Imagine what would happen if you could combine the power and speed of the rabbit with the steady finishing power of the turtle. What would happen if you mastered a simple set of principles to allow you to start fast and finish strong in each area of your life? What would happen if you had an action plan to help you turn your life from one of great *potential* to one of great *accomplishment?* You would make things happen. You would get ahead and stay ahead—no doubt about it!

SELF ASSESSMENT

1. What steps can you take to stop being a turtle—plodding along with marginal results? (Remember, beating the rabbit in this race is nothing to brag about.)

____

____

____

____

____

____

____

____

2. In what areas of your life have you resembled the rabbit—starting fast but failing to finish the race. What steps can you take to get out of a rabbit mindset?

____

____

____

____

____

____

____

____

3. List your strengths. List your weaknesses.

____

____

____

____

____

____

____

4. Based on your identified strengths and weaknesses, how can you restructure your strategy to improve your chances of success?

____

____

____

____

____

____

____

Are You satisfied with your current life strategy?
(cicle one)

Unsatisfied				**Uncertain**				**Satisfied**	
1	2	3	4	5	6	7	8	9	10

THINGS TO DO LIST

☑	Due Date	What can I do Today?

When you have completed your things to do list will you be satisfied with your current life strategy?

Unsatisfied				**Uncertain**					**Satisfied**
1	2	3	4	5	6	7	8	9	10

SECTION I

Assessing Your Position

When you plant a seed, don't envision a tree, envision a forest. —Unknown

CHAPTER 1

Recognizing Opportunity

Imagine reading the following help wanted ad in the local newspaper. Note: The names have been changed to protect the innocent, but people with the same profile can be found working in almost every organization.

Help Wanted: A four-person company owned by Everybody, Somebody, Anybody, and Nobody now hiring. Apply in person ***today!*** There was an important job to be done and Everybody was asked to do it. Anybody could have done it, but Nobody did it. Somebody got angry about that, because it was Everybody's job. Everybody thought Anybody could do it, but Nobody realized that Everybody wouldn't do it. Consequently, it wound up that Nobody told Anybody, so Everybody blamed Somebody. We need an organized person to get this job under control.

WOULD YOU CIRCLE THIS AD FOR FURTHER FOLLOW UP?

Looking at the ad more closely, do you think this job is a:

- ☐ Disaster waiting to happen?
- ☐ Place to work until something better comes along?
- ☐ Ground-floor opportunity?

As you have probably noticed, nothing is mentioned in the ad about what the actual position responsibilities entail—only that the ball has been dropped. But "anyone" could have done the job, so talent or skill must not be that important.

AN OPPORTUNITY OR NOT?

There are two factors you should consider when assessing whether or not this job would be an opportunity for you. First, is this a good company where you would want to work for the long term? If your answer is yes, the second question is for whom will you be working? Let's examine that question.

1. Will you work for Everybody? This company is looking for a person to do the work—or to blame if the work is not completed. If you work for Everybody, you will have many responsibilities, too many supervisors, and little direction. If you are willing to work for

Everybody and Everybody is your boss, you will have no room for growth. This dead end job is a disaster waiting to happen.

2. Will you work for Anybody? The position is deemed important, but the person doing it is not important ("Anybody could have done it"), so there is no growth potential. If you are willing to work for Anybody, you will find many takers and will invest a lot of time and effort for little compensation. This position is at best a place to work until something better comes along.

3. Will you work for Nobody? Working for Nobody means that you will be constantly working on rush projects as they were not noticed, assigned, or started until they were due. You can't get ahead working for Nobody, as Nobody will see your good work, and Nobody will pay you on payday! This position is a disaster waiting to happen.

4. Will you work for Somebody? Somebody is the person who got angry when an important project was not completed. You are being given an opportunity to solve Somebody's problem and keep others from blaming Somebody. Somebody should be willing to pay you well for this and other tasks Somebody may have. If you want to be a Somebody, you want to work for a Somebody. This is at least an attractive position to work at until something better comes along, and it may be a ground-floor opportunity.

Taking the time to select the right opportunities will allow you to make things happen in your life and cause you to move forward more rapidly.

SELF ASSESSMENT

1. Identify the Somebody's in your life.

____

____

____

____

____

____

____

2. Research the good places to work for the type of work you want to do. Consider local, national, and international companies. If none exist, it may be time to start your own company.

____

____

____

____

____

____

____

3. Who are the Somebody's you need to meet in your chosen life's path?

4. How will you go about meeting these Somebody's?

Who are you currently working for? (circle one)

Everybody			**Anybody**		**Nobody**			**Somebody**	
1	2	3	4	5	6	7	8	9	10

THINGS TO DO LIST

☑	Due Date	What can I do Today?

When you have completed your things to do list will you be working for?

Everybody			**Anybody**		**Nobody**			**Somebody**	
1	2	3	4	5	6	7	8	9	10

Chapter 2

Are You Ready for an Opportunity?

When my rich and eccentric Uncle Larry died recently, we all convened at his lawyer's office in New York City on Monday at 9 a.m. as requested. As each person's name was read, each was given an envelope. From their expressions, they were given instructions as strange as mine.

My letter read: Do not share this information with anyone in the room. Proceed at once by car, and by car only, to the First National Bank of San Diego, California. Your inheritance, a tidy sum, can be picked up by you, and you alone, at the main branch on or before Wednesday, close of business day.

I quickly pulled out my cell phone, punched in locations, and found that I had a 2,800-mile trip ahead of me, with approximately 43 hours of driving time. Looking at my watch, I had only 52 hours to complete the trip. This would certainly be a challenge.

WHAT WOULD YOU DO?

- ☐ Pass on this opportunity as a joke by quirky Uncle Larry.
- ☐ Determine that the task was impossible and go home cursing Uncle Larry all the way.
- ☐ Pass on the opportunity because of lack of time or money.
- ☐ Consider this an opportunity for adventure and profit.

I would choose opportunity. I love adventures and profit. My thought process: inventory my resources and make a quick check list while heading to my car—time was wasting.

My check list:

- ✓ Will my car make this trip? Or should I borrow or rent one that will get me to San Diego faster?
- ✓ Do I have enough identification on me to prove who I am at the bank? Should I go home to get additional identification? Could I have someone fax or mail

me identification somewhere along the way?

- ✓ Do I have a dependable GPS to show me the fastest way to San Diego and keep me on course.
- ✓ I know I can't drive 43 hours out of 52 hours. Who can I get to drive with me? Do I know any professional drivers? Two or three additional drivers would be even better.
- ✓ Do I have enough money to buy food and gas along the way?
- ✓ Is my cell phone charged so I can coordinate my activities while on the road?
- ✓ What is on my normal schedule that I may need to change?
- ✓ When does the bank close? Can I get the phone number online? Can I get them to stay open longer if needed?

Life can come at you fast! When an opportunity lands in your lap, you need to be aware of your current position, what resources are necessary, what resources are available, and finally to what resources you have access. Not knowing the answers to any of these questions may cost you an opportunity when it presents itself suddenly.

Three months after his death and two full months after I arrived home from a cruise, dearly departed Uncle Larry (it's amazing how an inheritance changed my perception of Uncle Larry) was at it again. From the grave this time, he issued another challenge—actually it was the same one. Drive from New York to San Diego in less than three days.

Considering your prior experience, would you be better:

- ☐ prepared for this challenge the second time?
- ☐ prepared if it happened a third time?
- ☐ able to pull your resources together?

If you were successful at the first challenge, you should now have enough money.

SELF ASSESSMENT

1. Looking back over your life, identify the opportunities that got away because you weren't prepared or lacked the resources.

2. List the specific items that caused you to pass on these opportunities.

3. Reviewing the list, have you sufficiently increased your preparedness and resources in case like opportunities present in the future?

____

____

____

____

____

____

____

____

4. How are you preparing for future opportunities?

____

____

____

____

____

____

____

____

Are you ready for an opportunity? (circle one)

Not ready			**Somewhat ready**					**Very ready**	
1	2	3	4	5	6	7	8	9	10

THINGS TO DO LIST

☑	Due Date	What can I do Today?

When you complete your things to do list will you be ready for an opportunity? (circle one)

Not ready			**Somewhat ready**					**Very ready**	
1	2	3	4	5	6	7	8	9	10

CHAPTER 3

Choosing Your Next Opportunity

One evening a warrior in a remote village began to prepare his son to face life as an adult with the inevitable afflictions and adversities he would face. The warrior told his son that all challenges ultimately are fought first between the two wolves inside him. One wolf is fear, which likes to take control of emotions and masquerades as lies, regret, feelings of inferiority, self-pity, envy, and anger. The other wolf is faith, consisting of trust, hope, joy, peace, humility, power, and love.

The son thought about the scenario for a few minutes—of two wolves battling against each other in his mind. He asked, "Which one wins, Dad?" The wise father simply said, "The one you feed."

WHICH WOLF ARE YOU FEEDING?

In this story, the father is suggesting that the son prepare himself to successfully manage future situations. Can we apply this same principle to future opportunities that we may encounter? Let's go back to high school for the answer.

Consider that:

- In gym class the best athlete was chosen first when putting together a team.
- The most attractive girl in class was asked to the dance first and the most often.
- The smartest students with the best grades had their choice of colleges to attend.

Would you agree that the best athlete, even though he may be physically gifted, probably worked hard at becoming a better athlete? In reality, the athlete prepared himself to be chosen first.

Would you agree that the most popular girl, while naturally attractive, worked hard at maintaining her appearance and mannerisms? In reality, she prepared herself to be the most popular.

Would you agree that the gifted students, while naturally intelligent, needed to work hard to maintain their grades? In reality, they prepared themselves to excel in their studies and to move successfully to the next level.

In each of these cases, these people used their natural gifts in conjunction with hard work to become their best at something, thereby separating them from the others. If we relate this to the initial story about the young warrior, the father was saying that the asset that is fed (athleticism, attractiveness, intelligence) develops into our strength.

In a competitive environment, it is easy to distinguish between one who shows up prepared every day and one who just shows up. As illustrated above, the person who is best prepared to make things happen usually gets the first and the most opportunities.

Let's take this example one step further: If you have an interest in a specific career field or particular industry and have enough talent to be gainfully employed in that area, why not inventory your skills, assess what you need to improve, and begin to hone your skill today. This way when an opportunity presents itself, you will be in the front of the line. In this way, *you* are choosing your next opportunity.

SELF ASSESSMENT

1. Think seriously about what do you do better than most people. Is there something you have always wanted to do better than anyone else?

____
____
____
____
____
____
____
____

2. Who are the people who need this product or service?

____
____
____
____
____
____
____
____

3. Would you consider this talent or skill to be consultant quality, professional quality, better than most, good enough to get by, or needs a lot of work? What steps can you take to make it consultant or professional quality?

____

____

____

____

____

____

____

____

4. What could you do now to hone each of these strengths to allow you to be first in line when an opportunity presents itself?

____

____

____

____

____

____

____

____

Have *you* decided on your next opportunity?
(circle one)

No				**Sort of**					**Yes!**
1	2	3	4	5	6	7	8	9	10

THINGS TO DO LIST

☑	Due Date	What can I do Today?

When you complete your things to do list will you have decided your next opportunity?

No				**Sort of**					**Yes!**
1	2	3	4	5	6	7	8	9	10

SECTION II

Attitudes for Opportunity

As he [a man] thinks in his heart, so is he.
—Proverbs 23:7 NKJV

CHAPTER 4

Optimism Is Contagious

John and Jake are 6-year-old twin boys, identical in almost every way except one. Their parents were worried that the boys had developed extreme personalities—John was a total pessimist, while Jake was a total optimist. Their parents decided to take them to a psychiatrist.

First the psychiatrist met with John the pessimist. Trying to brighten his outlook, the psychiatrist took him to a room piled to the ceiling with brand-new toys. But instead of yelping with delight, the little boy burst into tears.

"What's the matter?" the psychiatrist asked, baffled. "Don't you want to play with any of the toys?"

"Yes," the little boy bawled, "but if I did, I'd probably break them."

Next the psychiatrist met with Jake the optimist. Trying to dampen his outlook, the psychiatrist took him to a room piled to the ceiling with horse manure. But instead of wrinkling his nose in disgust, the optimist emitted the yelp of delight the psychiatrist had been hoping to hear from his brother, the pessimist. Then Jake clambered to the top of the pile, dropped to his knees, and began gleefully digging out scoop after scoop with his bare hands.

"What are you doing?" the psychiatrist asked, just as baffled by the optimist as he had been by the pessimist.

"With all this manure," the little boy replied, beaming, "there *must* be a pony in here somewhere!"

HOW DO YOU SEE THE WORLD?

Your attitude and outlook greatly determine your perception of the world and what others see when they look at you. In this chapter I want to focus on how other people perceive you. This is important because everyone wants to be around people who "fit in" with their ideals. For instance, to get into most clubs or organizations, you must be voted in.

Would you rather be with someone who is upbeat, positive, laughing, and forward thinking—or would you prefer to be around people who are always depressed, negative, frowning, and dwelling on past failed results?

Would you prefer to be with a person who only talks about him or herself—or a person who can talk about many subjects and equally shares a conversation?

Would you prefer to be with people with similar views or with people you have nothing in common?

Would you prefer to work with people who are always complaining—or people who purposefully attack the day's work and get their tasks completed quickly and efficiently?

The choices are obvious. The challenge is to become the type of person other people what to be around. As you become a more positive, upbeat person, you will find that you will attract other positive, upbeat people.

Pick people as friends and colleagues who present themselves as you would like to present yourself. What are they doing that you aren't doing? What changes can you make to come closer to what they do?

Model their actions and practice, Practice, PRACTICE.

SELF ASSESSMENT

1. List the areas of your life that are more negative than positive.

____
____
____
____
____
____
____
____

2. List what could be done to move each negative area toward the positive.

____
____
____
____
____
____
____
____

3. What areas lean more toward the positive than the negative?

____
____
____
____
____
____
____
____

4. Can these areas be improved in the same manner?

____
____
____
____
____
____
____
____

Are you a positive and optimistic person? (circle one)

Some Days				**Most Days**				**Every Day**	
1	2	3	4	5	6	7	8	9	10

THINGS TO DO LIST

☑	Due Date	What can I do Today?

When you complete your things to do list will you be a positive and optimistic person?

Some Days				**Most Days**				**Every Day**	
1	2	3	4	5	6	7	8	9	10

Chapter 5

Problem Versus Opportunity

When you wake up in the morning, do you see a day full of problems or a day full of opportunities? The following short quiz consists of four questions and reveals the truth about your style of thinking.

1. How do you put a giraffe into a refrigerator?

Correct Answer: Open the refrigerator, put the giraffe into the refrigerator, and close the door.

This question tests whether you tend to do simple things in an overly complicated way.

2. How do you put an elephant into a refrigerator?

Did you say, "Open the refrigerator, put in the elephant into the refrigerator, and close the refrigerator?" *(Wrong Answer.)*

Correct Answer: Open the refrigerator, take the giraffe out of the refrigerator, and put the elephant in the refrigerator and close the door.

This tests your ability to think through the repercussions of your previous actions.

3. The King of the Forest is hosting an animal conference. All the animals attend except one. Which animal does not attend?

Correct Answer: The Elephant. The elephant is in the refrigerator. You just put him in there.

This tests your memory.

4. There is a river you must cross but it is inhabited by crocodiles. How do you cross the river?

Correct Answer: You swim across. All the crocodiles are attending the animal conference.

This tests whether you learn quickly from your mistakes.

Note: According to Andersen Consulting Worldwide that created the quiz, 90 percent of the professionals tested gave the wrong answers. But many preschoolers got several correct answers. This seems to prove the theory that most professionals have the brains of a four-year-old.[1]

DEALING WITH PROBLEMS

When talking about problem solving, I believe there are four major categories of people.

First you have people that cause problems; this group soon finds they are being avoided by others

Second is the group that finds a problem and brings it to someone else. Lower level people want someone else to solve their problems.

Third is a group that recognizes a problem and takes it to the person that has the authority to solve the problem but at the same time takes a solution to that problem as well. Higher level people bring problems to people in charge but also bring a solution or two to solve the problem.

Fourth is the rare person who studies a situation, sees a potential opportunity, and takes steps to solve or minimize the effect of the problem before it happens.

Recognizing a problem is not difficult. Most people can do that. Finding effective solutions to problems is valuable to the person that owns the problem. Solving a problem before it costs time or money is a truly invaluable commodity.

As illustrated in the set of animal questions, even high level executives fail to recognize simple solutions to problems. The person who takes the time and can routinely locate and solve problems will make things happen and find limitless opportunities in many areas of life.

SELF ASSESSMENT

1. List the problems you encountered last week.

____

____

____

____

____

____

____

____

2. Were these problems resolved? What lessons can you learn from these situations that might apply to future situations?

____

____

____

____

____

____

____

____

3. Have there been times when you have had a solution to a problem but did not bring it to the table and someone else got the credit for solving the problem?

____

____

____

____

____

____

____

____

4. What current problems are you facing for which you can provide a solution and turn them into opportunities?

____

____

____

____

____

____

____

____

Are you a problem giver or a problem solver?
(circle one)

Problem Giver				**Both**			**Problem Solver**		
1	2	3	4	5	6	7	8	9	10

THINGS TO DO LIST

☑	Due Date	What can I do Today?

When you complete your list will you be a problem giver or a problem solver?

Problem Giver				**Both**			**Problem Solver**		
1	2	3	4	5	6	7	8	9	10

ENDNOTE

1. http://www.dclab.com/qualified_professional.asp; http://www.thinking-differently.com/2009/06/anderson-consulting-quiz/; accessed August 25, 2010.

CHAPTER 6

Adapting to Change

A very elderly lady looked in the mirror one morning. She had three remaining hairs on her head, and being a positive soul, she said, "I think I'll braid my hair today." So she braided her three hairs, and she had a great day.

Some days later, looking in the mirror one morning, preparing for her day, the lady saw that she had only two hairs remaining. "Hmm, two hairs. I fancy a center parting today." She duly parted her two hairs, and as ever, she had a great day.

A week or so later, the lady noticed that she had just one hair left on her head. "One hair, huh," she mused, "I know, a ponytail will be perfect." And again she had a great day.

The next morning she looked in the mirror. She was completely bald.

"Finally bald, huh," she said to herself, "How wonderful! I won't have to waste time styling my hair anymore."

COPING WITH LIFE

As in this illustration, most things that happen in life are not necessarily for or against you—they are simply things that happen. How you cope with life is how you perceive it. The lady certainly possessed a positive attitude about coping with the inevitable symptoms of old age.

If you view things as always being against you, you will:

- Be angry or upset most of the time.
- Waste much of your creative energy on getting even instead of using the same energy to move your agenda forward.
- Not view a situation as neutral and therefore work on a solution for your advancement. Instead, you will work on a way to shift the problem to another person, a waste of time.

Remember, accepting and solving problems is one way to get ahead.

Do you allow one bad thing to rob an hour, a morning, a day or more of your time?

Do you concentrate on the one bad thing that happens in a day or the ten good things?

GREAT UNCLE CLAUDE'S LESSON

When I was just getting started in business, my great uncle Claude was already well-established in the grocery business. At a family gathering after a very stressful week, I was ready to quit my job and move on. Then I heard a piece of advice that has helped me over and over throughout my life.

Great Uncle Claude said, "There are 21 working days in an average month. Two of those days will be so bad you will want to quit. However, two other days will be so good you will wonder why you would ever want to do anything else." Uncle Claude told me to do my planning during the remaining 17 days, which will be average days. This advice helped me keep perspective and from overstating or understating my position.

Before you pull out all of your hair, learn to average your problem(s) over a month, thereby leveling out the peaks and valleys that create stress.

SELF ASSESSMENT

1. List the problems that you experienced in your job or family this past week.

____

____

____

____

____

____

____

____

2. How did you adapt to each of these situations?

____

____

____

____

____

____

____

____

3. If you view problems as merely needing a solution and don't take them personally, can you develop better solutions?

____

____

____

____

____

____

____

____

4. How many problems are waiting for a creative thinker such as you?

____

____

____

____

____

____

____

____

How well do you roll with the punches? (circle one)

Never Roll			**Sometimes Roll**			**Consistent Roller**			
1	2	3	4	5	6	7	8	9	10

THINGS TO DO LIST

☑	Due Date	What can I do Today?

When you complete your Things to do list how well will you roll with the punches?

Never Roll			**Sometimes Roll**			**Consistent Roller**			
1	2	3	4	5	6	7	8	9	10

SECTION III

Organize for Opportunity

The organized person usually wins!
–Unknown

Chapter 7

Effective Communication

An old farmer trudges several miles through freezing snow to his local and very remote chapel for Sunday service. No one else is there, aside from the clergyman.

"I'm not sure it's worth proceeding with the service. Might we do better to go back to our warm homes and a hot drink?" asks the clergyman, inviting a mutually helpful reaction from his audience of one.

"Well, I'm just a simple farmer, but when I go to feed my herd, and if only one beast turns up, I sure don't leave it hungry."

So the clergyman, feeling somewhat ashamed, delivers his service with all the bells and whistles, hymns and readings, lasting a good couple of hours, finishing proudly with the fresh observation that no matter how small the need, our duty remains. And he thanks the farmer for the lesson he has learned.

"Was that okay?" asks the clergyman, as the two set off toward home.

"Well, I'm just a simple farmer, but when I go to feed my herd, and if only one beast turns up, I sure don't force it to eat what I brought for the whole herd…"

EATING AN ELEPHANT

No doubt you've heard the question and the answer: How do you eat an elephant? One bite at a time. The answer promises that even problems that appear too large for you to handle can be handled if you break them down to bite-size tasks and then complete one task at a time.

In a group, if everyone needs to know everything about a project, there is a redundancy of effort, which wastes a great deal of time and effort in communication.

A better plan is to first break down the project into bite-size pieces. Then organize the pieces into a logical order. Each person can then be given only what he or she needs to know with a slight overlap of information saving time and energy for more important tasks. Someone will then need to monitor the progress of the group and make sure everything is proceeding according to plan.

If you are in charge of breaking down the assignments, you need to get everyone working on their portion of the project and then tie up loose ends. The following four aspects of the process need to be considered:

1. What does each member of your team need?

2. How will each person best understand your communication? Verbal? Visual? Both?

3. Keep your instructions as simple as possible.

4. Don't beat a dead horse—don't repeat the assignments unless asked to do so.

SELF ASSESSMENT

1. When you *talk* to people, do they understand you or do they frequently ask you to clarify what you just said?

____

____

____

____

____

____

____

____

2. When you *write* to people, do they understand you or do they frequently ask you to clarify what you just said?

____

____

____

____

____

____

____

____

3. When you respond to questions, do you think about what you are going to say before you speak so that your response is easy to understand?

____

____

____

____

____

____

____

____

4. When you hand in a report, do you read over it several times to assure it is accurate and easily understood?

____

____

____

____

____

____

____

____

Rate your communication skills. (circle one)

Poor				**Average**				**Very Good**	
1	2	3	4	5	6	7	8	9	10

THINGS TO DO LIST

☑	Due Date	What can I do Today?

After you have completed your things to do list how will you communicate?

Poor				**Average**				**Very Good**	
1	2	3	4	5	6	7	8	9	10

Chapter 8

Time and Its Use

Following a poor first quarter performance, the board of Company X asked a senior manager to investigate what was happening on the factory floor. The directors believed poor productivity was at the root of the performance problem.

While walking around the plant, the investigating manager came upon a large warehouse area where a man stood next to a pillar. The manager introduced himself as the person investigating performance on the factory floor, and then asked the man by the pillar what he was doing. "It's my job," replied the man, "I was told to stand by this pillar."

The investigator thanked the man for his cooperation and encouraged him to keep up the good work. The investigator next walked into a large packing area, where he saw another man standing next to a pillar. The investigator again introduced himself and asked the man what he was doing. "I've been told to stand by this pillar, so that's what I do," said the man.

Two weeks later the investigator completed his report and duly presented his findings to the board, which held a brief meeting to decide remedial action. The board called the investigator back into the room, thanked him for his work, and then instructed him to fire one of the men he'd found standing by pillars—since obviously this was a duplication of effort.

UTILIZING TIME TO CREATE OPPORTUNITIES

Benjamin Franklin was quoted as saying a penny saved is a penny earned. This is tried, true, and valuable wisdom. Unlike money, time cannot be saved. You either invest it wisely or not, but either way it is gone.

You can, however, leverage time to provide value for you. This value may be in the form of increased sales, productivity, profits, leisure time, or whatever you want to have more of.

Imagine you and another person with similar qualifications start to work on the same day, doing the same job, for the same company. Everything about you and your counterpart is basically the same.

According to Salary.com., Americans waste more than two hours a day at work. If you and your counterpart each produced the average six hours of work, your employer may be satisfied. However, a simple strategy of working a full eight hours each day would allow you to out-produce your counterpart by 500 hours a year or more than 12 full weeks.

Another study found that one hour of planning can save up to four hours of time. Imagine if you were better at planning than your coworker, you could further increase your advantage. Are you getting the idea? You may be producing as much as 11 hours of work to his or her six hours of work, even though you have very similar skills.

By working smarter and managing your time, you could appear to be running circles around your counterpart. When advancement opportunities are presented, you would be in the front of the line.

If you find yourself holding up a pillar—or wasting time in other ways—you are holding yourself back from making good things happen in your life.

SELF ASSESSMENT

1. List the ways you waste time during the day. Simply logging your activities each day for a week is a good way to keep track.

____

____

____

____

____

____

____

____

2. Who causes you to waste time during the day? What conversations can you eliminate or cut short?

____

____

____

____

____

____

____

____

3. How do you plan your day? By the project? By the hour? By the minute? Is this the best way to plan?

4. What can you do to improve each of the above?

Rate your time management skills. (circle one)

Poor				**OK**				**Excellent**	
1	2	3	4	5	6	7	8	9	10

THINGS TO DO LIST

☑	Due Date	What can I do Today?

When you have completed your things to do list what will your management skills look like

Poor				**OK**				**Excellent**	
1	2	3	4	5	6	7	8	9	10

CHAPTER 9

Keep Accurate Records

An accountant dies and goes to Heaven. He reaches the pearly gates and is amazed to see a happy crowd all waving banners and chanting his name.

After a few minutes, Saint Peter comes running toward him and says, "I'm sorry I wasn't here to greet you personally. God is looking forward to meeting such a remarkable man as yourself."

The accountant is perplexed. "I've tried to lead a good life, but I am overwhelmed by your welcome," he tells Saint Peter.

"It's the least we can do for someone as special as you are. Imagine, living to the age of 123 and still looking so young," says Saint Peter.

The man looks even more dumbfounded and replies, "One hundred and twenty-three years old? I don't know what you mean. I'm only 40."

Saint Peter replies, "But that can't be right…we've seen your time sheets!"

OOPS! Bad record keeping!

Do you think this accountant's stock just plummeted from Saint Peter's perspective? Do you think he may be visiting a place with a distinctly hotter climate?

THE 250 RULE

I've worked in the printing industry for most of my life. Small printing companies often talk about the rule of 250, which states that every person talks to or directly affects the thinking of 250 other people. The rule of 250 came about because customers bought 250 birth announcements when they had a baby and 250 death announcements when someone died.

Imagine the business life of the accountant in our story. As he practiced what he deemed to be smart business by over-billing customers, he was actually burning bridges with thousands of people who impacted his future success.

You have a choice today. You can live by a set of principles that will impress people, and they will tell 250 friends—generating the goodwill necessary to greatly *increase* your success. Or you can live by a set of principles that will alienate people, and they will tell their 250 friends—generating conversation that will greatly *decrease* your chances of success.

The way you conduct your day-to-day activities may not be the difference between Heaven and hell. However, the higher you go in a company the more high level people you will come in contact with on a daily basis. Consider that there are many people with lower level positions in a company, but the higher the level, the fewer the people—meaning, one poor interaction with a high level executive can kill a career.

Before you find yourself in a position to be judged on something very important, determine who you are, how you want to be judged, and live your life that way every day.

SELF ASSESSMENT

1. Do you have a list of 250 friends and associates? Will these people lead you to good people and good opportunities and warn you to stay away from bad people and bad opportunities? If not, make a list of those who are looking out for your best interests and determine to keep in touch with them.

____

____

____

____

____

2. Make a list of people or companies you consider reputable. Make a list of people or companies with whom you would not consider doing business. Are you letting your "250" know?

____

____

____

____

____

3. Are there areas in your life you need to clean up? List them, and clean them up before they cost you time or money.

____

____

____

____

____

____

____

____

4. Are there bridges you need to rebuild? List them, and rebuild them to limit the damage.

____

____

____

____

____

____

____

____

Do you have 250 people you can count on? (circle one)

No Way				**Maybe**					**Yes**
1	2	3	4	5	6	7	8	9	10

THINGS TO DO LIST

☑	Due Date	What can I do Today?

After you have completed your things to do list will you have 250 people you can count on?

No Way				**Maybe**					**Yes**
1	2	3	4	5	6	7	8	9	10

SECTION IV

Prepare Your Team for Opportunity

Team building is the art of maximizing time by using other people's time.

CHAPTER 10

Individual Versus Team

An out of towner drove his car into a ditch in a desolated area. Luckily, a local farmer came to help with his big, strong horse named Buddy.

He hitched up Buddy to the car and yelled, "Pull, Nellie, pull." Buddy didn't move.

Then the farmer hollered, "Pull, Buster, pull." Buddy didn't respond.

Once more the farmer commanded, "Pull, Jennie, pull." Nothing.

Then the farmer nonchalantly said, "Pull, Buddy, pull." And the horse easily dragged the car out of the ditch.

The motorist was most appreciative but very curious. He asked the farmer why he called his horse by the wrong name three times.

The farmer said, "Oh, Buddy is blind, and if he thought he was the only one pulling, he wouldn't even try!"

WHO IS ON YOUR TEAM?

Your team can and should include anyone you interact with on an ongoing basis. Family, friends, associates, co-workers, shop owners, and club members are just a few who come quickly to mind. Why is it important to identify your team? A good team will beat a great individual almost every time.

Creating a team is the same as creating any relationship, you get out of it what you put in to it. To have a great team you need to be a great team member.

Did you know that a two-horse team, as suggested in the story, will pull more than twice the weight as a single horse can pull? The same is true with people. You will find that the people who are part of and contribute to a larger and more organized team are offered more opportunities.

What are the differences between a good team and a poor team? What should you be giving to a team and expecting in return?

A GREAT TEAM IS:	A POOR TEAM IS:
Based on trust	Based on distrust
Unconditional in nature	Conditional in nature
Based on giving of self	Based on growth of self
Predicated on relationships	Predicated on results
Made at arms embrace	Made at arms length
One that asks, What am I bringing to the team?	One that asks, What am I getting from this team?
Enforced by character	Enforced by court
Bound by loyalty	Bound by leverage
Commitment-based	Convenience-based
A want-to commitment	A have-to commitment
Forever	For a specified period
Welcoming; nobody wants to leave	Defining; nobody leaves until the terms are met.

SELF ASSESSMENT

1. Conduct an official, or unofficial, study of the skills for each member of your team. Record the results and devise ways to improve interaction.

____

____

____

____

____

____

____

____

2. List the skills your team is missing.

____

____

____

____

____

____

____

____

3. Who do you know that has these skills?

____

____

____

____

____

____

____

____

4. How can you meet and recruit these people for your team?

____

____

____

____

____

____

____

____

How would you rate your team? (circle one)

What team?				**Good**					**Excellent**
1	2	3	4	5	6	7	8	9	10

THINGS TO DO LIST

☑	Due Date	What can I do Today?

After you have completed your things to do list how will your team shape up?

What team?				**Good**				**Excellent**	
1	2	3	4	5	6	7	8	9	10

Chapter 11

Build a Team

About Crows
by John Ciardi

The old crow is getting slow,
the young crow is not.
Of what the young crow does not know,
the old crow knows a lot.

At knowing things, the old crow is still
the young crow's master.
What does the old crow not know?
How to go faster.

The young crow flies above, below, and rings around
the slow old crow.
What does the fast young crow not know?
Where to go.

VALUE

Who is the more valuable team member?

If you were assembling a team, who would you select—the old crow or the young crow? The answer depends on the task that needs to be completed.

What would happen if there were ten crows to choose from, each with a different skill set. Which crow would you choose? The same answer—it depends on the task to be completed.

Consider that the shortest distance between two points is a straight line. If you knew your final destination, you would choose a straight line, assemble a team that would get you to your destination most efficiently, then never waver from your course.

However, life is seldom about well-structured straight lines. In fact, much of the "quality of life" people talk about is experiencing new and exciting things that are off the straight-line path. Sometimes you need to get to point A before you see point B that is slightly to the right. Then when you get to point B, you see point C that is way over to the left, and so on.

Which team will best be able to help you get to a future point(s) when you don't know where that point(s) is yet? Choose team members that you like, are smart, flexible, have varied skill sets, and are great problem solvers. In that way, you will be prepared for as many eventualities as possible and with people you enjoy being around.

ASSIGNING TASKS

After breaking down a project into tasks, as discussed in a previous chapter, you need to utilize your team and resources to handle each and every task.

In life we measure the worth of what we are ready to invest in by value. A way to determine value is to evaluate the traits of quality, price, and service. The same is true of assigning tasks.

Consider that if you need a project completed quickly, you may pick a dependable person to do the project. But if you need the same project completed very precisely, you may select another person on your team. And if you need the project developed and presented, you may select still another team member.

Learning to mesh team members' skills with the appropriate task to achieve your objective is what makes or breaks a project's success.

SELF ASSESSMENT

1. Take the time to list the "plus level" skill of each of your team members.

2. Take the time to get input from your team before making assignments.

3. Do you know the potential holes in your team's talent pool? Are you prepared to outsource (extended team) certain work when necessary?

____

____

____

____

____

____

____

____

4. If you get an influx of work and your team gets overloaded, do you have outsourcing (extended team) available to handle the extra work?

____

____

____

____

____

____

____

____

How good are you at choosing a team? (circle one)

Not Good				**Average**				**Very Good**	
1	2	3	4	5	6	7	8	9	10

THINGS TO DO LIST

☑	Due Date	What can I do Today?

After you have completed your things to do list how good will you be at choosing a team?

Not Good				**Average**				**Very Good**	
1	2	3	4	5	6	7	8	9	10

CHAPTER 12

Coaching

One day a traveler, walking along a lane, came across three stonecutters working in a quarry. Each was busy cutting a block of stone. Interested to find out what they were working on, he asked the first stonecutter what he was doing. "I am cutting a stone!"

Still no wiser, the traveler turned to the second stonecutter and asked him what he was doing. "I am cutting this block of stone to make sure that it's square, and its dimensions are uniform, so that it will fit exactly in its place in a wall."

A bit closer to finding out what the stonecutters were working on but still unclear, the traveler turned to the third stonecutter. He seemed to be the happiest of the three and when asked what he was doing, the stonecutter replied, "I am building a cathedral."1

DEVELOPING PEOPLE

Do you remember when you were young and drew a picture by connecting the dots? You simply found point one and then connected it to point two and then to point three. When you got to the last numbered dot you had drawn a picture.

Life is often more complex than just connecting the dots, as they say. In life you don't always know where all of the dots are, and when you locate them, they are not numbered sequentially.

If you are leading a team, you have already determined how to solve problems and have probably demonstrated that you are good at problem solving. However, to be a good leader, you must also be good at showing your *team* how to solve problems by seeing them from a different perspective.

You can chose to develop team members to think for themselves, or you can chose to teach your team to run to you for each and every answer they need.

When team members can think for themselves, it allows you to manage many more people; and the more people you can manage, the higher you can go in an organization.

Let's consider the following four-step approach:

1. Teach your team to locate the dots. This includes things that need to be completed, available resources, due dates, budgets, etc.

2. Teach your team to see the relationship between the dots. What step leads to what result, leads to what next step, etc.

3. Teach your team to number the dots so that connecting them creates a picture—a workable solution to reach the goal.

4. Finally, teach your team to continually rework the numbers to see if there is a better picture that can be made—a better solution to reaching the goal.

The better your team members are at the four steps, the more work your team will accomplish. The greater their success, the more the team and the team leader—you—will be given opportunities to move to positions of greater authority. Making things happen is how to succeed!

SELF ASSESSMENT

1. Establish a training program for each member of your team.

2. Allow each team member to feel as if he or she is "building a cathedral" to create an attitude of motivation.

3. List ways you can pull your team up to your level.

4. Are you continuing to do things the same way, or are you reworking the dots to create efficiencies?

How good are you as a coach?

Not Good				**OK**				**Very Good**	
1	2	3	4	5	6	7	8	9	10

THINGS TO DO LIST

☑	Due Date	What can I do Today?

After finishing your things to do list how good of a coach will you be?

Not Good				**Average**				**Very Good**	
1	2	3	4	5	6	7	8	9	10

ENDNOTE

1. http://www.the-happy-manager.com/leadership-quality.html; accessed August 25, 2010.

Conclusion

Your 21-Day Challenge

Remember the transcript between U.S. naval ship and the Canadian authorities that you read in the Preface? Remember how the Americans were being told to change course to avoid a collision? Well, now that you are armed with all the proven successful strategies provided in this book, I am encouraging you to set your course to one that will take you on a journey toward fulfilling your unique destiny.

HOW TO MISS THE LIGHTHOUSE

It only takes 21 well-planned and executed days to establish or change a habit. Simply making a small change from one of the chapters during each 21-day period will help you get ahead and stay ahead, now that you know the art of making things happen in your life.

As you complete each 21 days, don't forget to date the form, as you will undoubtedly notice changes over the weeks and months ahead. And periodically reviewing the form and your answers will help you stay on course when you run into those inevitable storms.

Good luck and good sailing!

21-DAY CHALLENGE

Date started ___________ Date ended___________

1. Fill in your self-evaluation from the end of each chapter.

2. Identify which chapters need the first and most attention.

3. Target a small improvement.

4. At the end of 21 days, conduct another self-evaluation.

5. Target another small improvement.

	Self-evaluation 1-10	Action to take to make things happen	21-day self-evaluation
Introduction			
Chapter 1			
2			
3			
4			
5			
6			
7			
8			
9			
10			
11			
12			
Total			

21-DAY CHALLENGE

Date started ___________ Date ended____________

1. Fill in your self-evaluation from the end of each chapter.

2. Identify which chapters need the first and most attention.

3. Target a small improvement.

4. At the end of 21 days, conduct another self-evaluation.

5. Target another small improvement.

	Self-evaluation 1-10	Action to take to make things happen	21-day self-evaluation
Introduction			
Chapter 1			
2			
3			
4			
5			
6			
7			
8			
9			
10			
11			
12			
Total			

For more information visit:
www.DeanDrawbaugh.com